Steam on the Settle & Carlisle

Compiled by David Joy

Dalesman Books
1981

The Dalesman Publishing Company Ltd.,
Clapham (via Lancaster), North Yorkshire LA2 8EB
First published 1981
© Text, Dalesman Publishing Company Ltd., 1981
ISBN: 0 85206 648 1

Printed in Great Britain by Fretwell & Brian Ltd.,
Howden Hall, Howden Road, Silsden, Keighley, West Yorkshire

Contents

Foreword 5

Return of Steam (by Peter Fox) 6

The Long Drag: Settle Junction to Blea Moor 10

Between the Tunnels: Blea Moor to Rise Hill 24

Over the Top: Garsdale and Ais Gill 32

The Eden Valley: Mallerstang to Carlisle 50

Vintage Steam 64

Cover illustrations:
Front: Stanier 4-6-2 No. 46229 'Duchess of Hamilton' near Appleby with the up Cumbrian Mountain Express on March 28th, 1981 *(D. Morris)*.
Back: A Jubilee 4-6-0 passes Ais Gill summit with an up express *(Eric Treacy)*.

CUMBRIAN
MOUNTAIN
EXPRESS
5690
LMS

Foreword

WE must be thankful that in the 1980s the Settle & Carlisle is still there at all. It has become one of the great survivors, clinging on to life against seemingly insuperable odds. By all logic its traffic should long since have been diverted to more kindly routes, both easier to operate and less expensive to maintain. This wildly improbable main line across the high Pennines could then have been left to crumble and decay, its magnificent viaducts and tunnels forming a linear archaeological attraction that might ultimately be seen in the same league as Hadrian's Wall.

Instead, the Settle & Carlisle has produced yet another surprise — and one that only a few years ago would have seemed beyond the wildest dreams. Now that steam has returned from the grave and triumphantly reappeared on the tracks of British Rail, the line has become one of the most splendid of all settings for witnessing preserved locomotives at work in weather both fair and — more usually — foul.

Yet this could well be the grand finale. British Rail has at last made public its fears for the structural stability of Ribblehead viaduct and has prepared contingency plans on the basis that it could become unsafe for traffic in as short a time as three years. The cost of a replacement has been put at £4½ million and it seems inconceivable that the line's capacity for self-preservation should triumph over expenditure of such magnitude.

The following pages therefore form a possible valedictory tribute to steam's final fling on the Settle & Carlisle, concentrating on the Cumbrian Mountain Express and other specials which have pounded their way over Ais Gill since the spring of 1978. In response to continuing demand, a selection of pre-1968 'vintage steam' photographs, several originally published in the Dalesman book 'Settle–Carlisle Centenary' in 1975, have also been included.

I should particularly like to thank the various photographers — and especially Peter Fox who also penned the introduction — for braving the elements and producing such memorable results in the face of climatic adversity.

— David Joy
July 1981

Opposite: The Settle & Carlisle personified. 'Leander' takes the up Cumbrian Mountain Express through Dent on July 3rd, 1980. (G. W. Morrison)

Return of Steam

by Peter Fox

THERE is a railway line in England which strides its way over the Pennine fells, linking north to south; Carlisle to Settle. This is a line which in the 1870s was constructed skilfully by railway engineers across the rugged contours of wild moorland, high fells and beautiful dales, climbing through a ruling gradient of 1 in 100 from near sea level to 1169ft at Ais Gill. It is a line full of names of interest and resonance: Horton-in-Ribblesdale, Selside, Batty Moss, Blea Moor, Pen-y-ghent, Arten Gill, Dandry Mire, Ais Gill, Lunds, Mallerstang, to name but a few. Indeed, the railwaymen themselves christened the line the 'Long Drag'. It is a line of solitude, where the sounds of steam can blend with the howl of the wind or the bleating of sheep.

All too late I discovered that despite, and sometimes because of, its varying weathers, the Settle–Carlisle line with steam power was a happy hunting-ground and most photogenic as well. Along with many others at the time, I refused to believe that British Rail really meant it when they spoke of the demise of steam. Yet on August 11th, 1968, along with thousands of others, I witnessed 'the last steam train' on British rails leaving Blea Moor hauled by two of Stanier's Class 5 locomotives 44781 and 44871. Was this really to be the end of main-line steam? Sadly all believed it was to be so. The '70s came and dwindled on with steam enthusiasts forced to turn their attention to the preserved lines.

In 1976 the centenary of the opening of the line was celebrated in fine style, especially by the running of centenary specials over the route. Many had hoped that the trains would be steam hauled. This was not allowed and the specials were diesel hauled, yet B.R. did allow two steam locomotives, L.N.W.R. 790 'Hardwicke' and L.N.E.R. 4472 'Flying Scotsman', to run to the southern end of the line at Settle. Despite typically wet Pennine weather on the day, 790 and 4472 remained in the siding at Settle for most of the afternoon, to the delight of the thousands who ignored the weather. These centenary celebrations showed that there was considerable nostalgic interest on the part of the general public as well as the enthusiast in steam-hauled trains as well as in the Settle–Carlisle route.

Ten years after the last steam train ran, B.R. changed its mind and agreed to a limited return of steam specials to the Settle–Carlisle line in 1978. Was this to be the beginning of a renewal for Settle–Carlisle steam in the ensuing years? Was I after all to have a second chance? Fortuitously it has turned out to be so but all did not go well at first.

Together with many hundreds of people, I positioned myself complete with camera at Ribblehead viaduct for the first return of steam to this route in March 1978. But the Pennine weather, true to form, conspired to produce its worst and L.N.E.R. 4771 'Green Arrow' was glimpsed hurrying across the viaduct like a shadow, against the misty 'white-out' of driving snow. Nevertheless the sight and sound of steam was back on the 'Long Drag'. Some weeks later saw the B.R. 9F 'Evening Star', No.92220, hauling another special over the line on 13th May, 1978. Sadly, one of the finest of railway photographers and Settle–Carlisle enthusiast, Bishop Eric Treacy, died at Appleby station whilst awaiting this special. As a tribute to this man B.R. ran two steam specials in his honour on September 30th, 1978 and named them 'The Lord Bishop' and 'The Bishop Treacy'.

Further complications arose in 1979. As a result of the diversions necessitated over the line because of the tunnel collapse at Penmanshiel on the East Coast main line, the planned steam specials for that year were cancelled for the Settle–Carlisle route.

Then in the early months of 1980, thanks to the tireless efforts of the Steam Locomotive Operators' Association (S.L.O.A.) and the co-operation of British Rail, a train to be called the Cumbrian Mountain Express was introduced to run both north and south over the Settle–Carlisle line, using the electrified route of the west coast to complete the circular tour. This eventually produced more steam on the line than since its closure to steam in 1968. Truly a 'second coming' had dawned for steam and the Settle–Carlisle. Originally there were to be six trains, three northbound and three southbound between 19 January and 22 March, 1980. Demand was so great in fact, that the number of trains run was doubled and the workings continued until Saturday, April 19th, finally culminating the following weekend, April 26th, with a return run on the one day by L.M.S. 5XP 5690 'Leander'.

Typically these days and runs enabled the photographer to sample the best and worst of the weather in the high fells, and one cannot but feel that the inhabitants of the dales must have become quite used to the weekly influx of enthusiasts on Saturdays. The writer recalls being asked by one farmer on a tractor, 'Be summat 'appening then?', as his farm lane became congested with what must have appeared like some sort of car rally as the photographers moved on to their next vantage point.

The Cumbrian Mountain Express ran in two 'legs', first from Carnforth to Skipton and then Skipton to Carlisle, northbound, and the following week in reverse order, southbound, with the steam locomotive being 'shedded' at Carlisle for the intervening week. The ex-L.M.S. Black 5 No. 5305, in superb condition, from Mr. Draper at Hull, ran on no less than ten of these first Cumbrian Mountain Expresses. This was surely fitting for this ex-L.M.S. route. Ex-L.N.E.R. No. 4472 'Flying Scotsman' and 4498 'Sir Nigel Gresley' shared the journeys with 5305, whilst ex-L.M.S. Jubilee No. 5690 'Leander' ran on the last two of the winter Cumbrian Mountain Expresses. All these locomotives put up some sterling and memorable performances. Apart from the normal stops necessitated by locomotive changes, the C.M.E. tours allowed photographic stops at Dent, Garsdale, and Appleby, northbound, and at Appleby and Garsdale, southbound. Such was the locomotive performance on the early tours that a southbound stop was soon added at Ribblehead and one at Armathwaite northbound. The real virtue of the Settle–Carlisle line for steam operation is that on Saturday afternoons there is a gap of five hours between passenger trains and no freight trains which allows great freedom for long stops and manoeuvres by steam workings.

The journeys themselves were often quite eventful. The southbound C.M.E.s had to be shunted onto the North Eastern exchange line at Appleby in order to allow the 11.50 Glasgow–Nottingham to pass; upon occasions, too, the C.M.E. had to be shunted on to the 'wrong line' to allow a delayed train to pass. On another occasion the C.M.E. had to be diverted into the loop at Blea Moor so as to allow a replacement D.M.U. to pass, because of engineering works at Skipton.

For myself, one of the highlights of the winter 1980 C.M.E.s occurred on the 22nd March. I had driven north through blizzards to Ais Gill and waited patiently for the overdue C.M.E., with fingers almost frozen to the camera. All round was whiteness, falling snow and silence; little could be seen and my mind thought back to a similar day in 1978. But suddenly one could hear the staccato exhaust beat of 5305 climbing up through Mallerstang and suddenly the snow ceased; the sun broke through into brilliant blue patches of sky just at the moment when 5305 came thundering past on her climb to the summit. The scene became one of instant incredible beauty; the steaming exhaust of 5305 became at one with the glories of nature in the high fells. Many exciting photographs were taken in those ensuing seconds by those fortunate to be there. For me it was well worth the hardships endured — for the scenic splendour of the Settle–Carlisle route truly came into its own.

Such was the success of the winter C.M.E.s that B.R. decided to run Cumbrian Mountain Expresses during the summer months of 1980, southbound only as a tourist service for the general public rather than especially for the enthusiast. This was to be a complementary service to the already well-proven Cumbrian Coast Express. The locomotive from the C.C.E. upon arrival at Ravenglass worked on to Carlisle and then two days later hauled the C.M.E. from Carlisle to Skipton; another steam locomotive then completed the journey from Skipton to Carnforth. In addition to L.N.E.R. 4472, L.N.E.R. 4498 and L.M.S. 5690, Steamtown included ex-S.R. 850 'Lord Nelson'. 850 was hastily

restored to main-line running order just in time for the 'Rocket 150' celebrations in May 1980 and from then onwards the 'Lord' showed his paces over the 'Long Drag' on several of the summer 1980 Cumbrian Mountain Expresses. Ex-L.M.S. 4–6–2 6201 'Princess Elizabeth' also spent a few weeks among the 'royalty' at Steamtown during the summer and hauled the C.M.E. upon a couple of occasions.

Although only southbound trains were run the C.M.E.s were well patronised by the public, despite the indifferent summer weather. On Thursday, 21st August, 1980, there occurred one of the minor dramas to which railways are accustomed, which involved the C.M.E. On that particular afternoon I was waiting just south of Ais Gill, along with many other photographers and enthusiasts. About half an hour before the C.M.E. was due, a southbound mixed freight passed, hauled by a Class 40 diesel. All seemed to be well. However the expected arrival time of the C.M.E. at Ais Gill came and went, but still no train!—when suddenly, instead of the expected, pluming exhaust down Mallerstang valley, there appeared but faint wisps of white steam approaching very slowly towards Ais Gill. It was a steam locomotive, but not working hard against the grade. Silence fell as everyone, cameraman and sound recordist alike, noted the slow passing of ex-L.M.S. 5690 'Leander', heading south, light engine *and* working wrong line! Clearly something was amiss. Where was the C.M.E. itself? I raced for the car and quickly followed 'Leander' to Lunds viaduct and then to Garsdale. At the approaches to Garsdale, standing silently complete with goods train, was the Class 40 — it had failed! The reason for the ghost-like appearance of 'Leander' was now apparent. Steam was about to rescue diesel! The sun poured down from a summer sky, giving us all perfect conditions to witness and record 'the Leander incident' as it has become known in railway circles. Here was 5690 on her last run before departing to the Severn Valley Railway for overhaul, pulling a distressed B.R. train into Garsdale and shunting it into the safety of the sidings. 5690 hurried back to Kirkby Stephen to rejoin her C.M.E. train and then came again up the incline at Ais Gill, this time with the full roar of her Jubilee exhaust and of course much later than advertised.

I relate this incident in some detail, because it does reveal that the steam locomotive photographer is truly at the moment enjoying a 'second coming' as far as main-line steam is concerned. Not recording what has been missed but recording and enjoying the new workings and incidents of a new 'steam era' — long may it last!

Encouraged by the success of the 1980 C.M.E. tours over the Settle–Carlisle line, British Rail and the S.L.O.A. arranged a programme of 1980/81 winter C.M.E.s. Not as many were planned or actually run as in 1980, because S.L.O.A. diversified, introducing the 'Welsh Marches Express' on the alternate Saturdays to the C.M.E. Nevertheless, the 1981 winter C.M.E.s involved different and interesting locomotives, including two ex-L.M.S. Black Fives, Stanier's mixed traffic design, 4767 and 5407. 4767 'George Stephenson' came down to Steamtown from the North Yorkshire Moors Railway to join 5407; both were resplendent in different L.M.S. liveries, 5407 in pre-war lined black and 4767 in the post-war black livery. These two were joined by another famous ex-L.M.S. locomotive, the 'Pacific' 4–6–2 46229 'Duchess of Hamilton' restored in crimson B.R. livery. Unfortunately the weather was not too kind on the days when the 'Duchess' hauled the C.M.E.s but she made a memorable sight as, clad in rich maroon, she climbed from the green backcloth of the Ribble valley up into the browns, russets, purples and greys of the high fells and moorlands of Blea Moor and Wild Boar Fell and then down into the lush greens of the Eden valley.

Poetic justice occurred, some may say, when on her first northbound run 46229 had to be assisted at the rear of the train by a Class 40 because of lack of adhesion due to greasy, autumn leaf-covered rails! The final winter northbound C.M.E. was double-headed by the Black Fives 4767 and 5407. Some spectacular exhaust patterns were produced by this pair, especially on the climb over Ribblehead. One other innovation occurred during the running of the winter C.M.E.s; this was the introduction by B.R. of 'run pasts'. This allowed the passengers on the C.M.E. to disembark, suitably position themselves and then take photographs of the locomotive and train in action. These 'run pasts' have usually taken place at Appleby and Garsdale. In all cases the firemen responded to the call by coaling up the fire, which produced some rich, claggy, high skybound combinations of smoke and steam.

Finally in April 1981, S.L.O.A. purchased a train of Pullman coaches and the last winter C.M.E. used these coaches and became instead the first Cumbrian Mountain Pullman. 5407 hauled this train from Carlisle to Skipton, complete with some spectacular run pasts, in a style well worthy of this former L.M.S. locomotive.

Despite the problems associated with this Settle–Carlisle line, and especially the crumbling Ribblehead viaduct, the steam trains *must* continue and the line *must* remain open. They provide considerable revenue for B.R. as well as leisure and pleasure for thousands of people . . . and why shouldn't this be so? Happily, B.R. is again running summer C.M.E.s over the Settle & Carlisle in 1982. Perhaps my personal view and recollections will stimulate interest in others in main-line scenic steam and who knows may allow them to become infected with that plague of the high fells — the disease of Settle–Carlisleitis!

The Long Drag

Settle Junction to Blea Moor

Scenes at Settle Junction. Above: 'Hardwicke' and 'Evening Star' on the Locomotive Club of Great Britain 'Fells & Dales' rail-tour — the former engine featured in the line's centenary celebrations at Settle in May 1976. *(J. C. Marsh).*

Opposite: 'Flying Scotsman' en route to Carlisle on March 29th, 1980. *(G. W. Morrison)*

The Citadel Express of September 23rd, 1978, hauled by Merchant Navy Pacific No. 35028 'Clan Line', crosses Sheriff Brow bridge on the climb to Ribblehead. *(J. C. Marsh)*

9F 2-10-0 No. 92220 'Evening Star' forges its way up the Long Drag with The Border Venturer on May 13th, 1978. This was the first appearance of a 9F on the line since 1968 — when 'Evening Star' was only eight years old. It was while waiting to photograph this train at Appleby that Bishop Eric Treacy, one of the finest of railway photographers, collapsed and died. *(Gordon Findlay)*

The return of steam to the Settle & Carlisle on March 25th, 1978, after an absence of ten years was, perhaps appropriately, marked by blizzard conditions. V2 No. 4771 'Green Arrow' pounds out of Sheriff Brow cutting in a virtual white-out. *(J. C. Marsh)*

At Helwith Bridge. Above: 5MT No. 4767 'George Stephenson', in post-war unlined black livery, steams past the snowy slopes of Pen-y-ghent on February 21st, 1981.

Opposite: Almost a year earlier, on March 29th, 1980, 'Flying Scotsman' is in charge of a ten-coach Cumbrian Mountain Express. *(both G. W. Morrison)*

THE
BISHOP
TREACY

Right: The York - Carlisle Citadel Express almost at cloud level as it approaches Ribblehead station.
(J. C. Marsh)

Opposite: 'Evening Star' struggles past Horton-in-Ribblesdale with The Bishop Treacy memorial special on September 30th, 1978.
(G. W. Morrison)

The majesty of Ribblehead. Left: A4 No. 4498 'Sir Nigel Gresley' restarts after making a stop with the Cumbrian Mountain Express on January 26th, 1980.

Right: 'Flying Scotsman', blowing a full head of steam into the mountain air, makes an unexpected halt at the north end of the viaduct. *(both Peter Fox)*

Bird's eye view of Ribblehead viaduct. In 1981 British Rail at last made public the information that this magnificent structure is crumbling away and could become unsafe for traffic within less than three years. *(Tom Parker)*

Whernside totally dwarfs one of the few double-headed Cumbrian Mountain Expresses as 5MT 4-6-0s Nos. 4767 and 5407 leave a fine smoke trail as they head for Blea Moor. *(Peter Fox)*

Two classic steam scenes on Ribblehead viaduct with 5MT No. 5305 in fine form in March 1980. Repair work on the viaduct is clearly in evidence in the upper photograph. *(Peter Fox)*

'Flying Scotsman' surmounts the Long Drag. Below: Passing Ribblehead station on March 29th, 1980.

Opposite: Heading towards Blea Moor box after crossing Ribblehead viaduct with the Bishop Treacy special on September 30th, 1978. *(both G. W. Morrison)*

4472
L N E R

Between the Tunnels

Blea Moor to Rise Hill

Above: Driver's eye view from the dark interior of Blea Moor tunnel.
(Geoffrey G. Hoare)

Opposite: 5XP 4-6-0 No. 5690 'Leander' emerges from the north portal of Blea Moor on April 26th, 1980. Note how coniferous afforestation is transforming the upper reaches of the Settle & Carlisle. *(G. W. Morrison)*

LMS
5690

Arten Gill viaduct. Above: Ex Southern Railway 4-6-0 No. 850 'Lord Nelson' joined the ranks of locomotives working the Cumbrian Mountain Express in the summer of 1980; it is seen here on July 31st. *(David Wilcock).*

Opposite: 'Flying Scotsman', viewed from the floor of Dentdale on March 29th, 1980, and looking very much like a toy train. *(G. W. Morrison)*

CUMBRIAN MOUNTAIN EXPRESS
Passengers must not cross the line
850

Contrasting locomotives in precisely the same location at the north end of Dent station. Above: 4-6-2 No. 6201 'Princess Elizabeth' in magnificent condition on September 4th, 1980.

Opposite: Minutes before it was photographed at Arten Gill (see page 26), 'Lord Nelson' hurries south on July 31st, 1980. *(both G. W. Morrison)*

Hull-based 5MT No. 5305, a popular and volatile performer on the Settle & Carlisle in 1980, pauses at Dent for a photographic stop on March 15th. *(David Wilcock)*

The driver has a clear view of Arten Gill viaduct as 5MT No. 5407 clears Dent with the inaugural Cumbrian Mountain Pullman on May 2nd, 1981. *(Peter Fox)*

On the cold and clear March 1st, 1980, No. 5305 heads through the cutting north of Dent station. *(J. C. Marsh)*

Over the Top

Garsdale and Ais Gill

Above: Ex North British 0-6-0 No. 673 'Maude' pauses at Garsdale on May 24th, 1980, en route to the 'Rocket 150' celebrations at Rainhill. The dry weather conditions meant driving had to be light-handed, leading to much accumulation of cinder in the smokebox — hence periodic stops for raking out. *(Gordon Findlay).*

Opposite: 'Evening Star' stops to take water with the northbound Border Venturer on May 13th, 1978. *(Derek Cross)*

Steam to the rescue! The so-called 'Leander incident' of August 21st, 1980, when 5XP No. 5690 was commandeered off the Cumbrian Mountain Express to remove a failed class 40 diesel and its freight train which were obstructing the up main line just north of Garsdale. Here the combined equipage moves into the station prior to reversing into one of the seldom-used sidings. *(Peter Fox)*

Earlier, 'Leander' had worked wrong-line from Kirkby Stephen to Garsdale to reach the front end of the failed diesel. Its appearance at Ais Gill caused much surprise among the waiting photographers (above). With its rescue mission completed, the locomotive returned to Kirkby Stephen and finally appeared once more with the now much delayed Cumbrian Mountain Express.
(both Peter Fox)

An innovation on the British Rail winter specials of 1980/1 was the introduction of 'run-pasts', allowing passengers to disembark and photograph the train. Firemen have regarded the operation as a challenge, coaling up the fire in order to produce some rich, claggy, high skybound combinations of smoke and steam as spectacularly demonstrated at Garsdale on May 2nd, 1981. *(Peter Fox)*

Following the purchase of a train of Pullman coaches by the Steam Locomotive Operators' Association, the last Cumbrian Mountain Express of winter 1980/1 in fact became the first Cumbrian Mountain Pullman. Here 5MT No. 5407 takes a well-earned rest at Garsdale on May 2nd after indulging in the pyrotechnics shown opposite. *(Peter Fox)*

Above: The Settle & Carlisle holds a special affection for inspector George Gordon, here seen in the cab of 'Duchess of Hamilton' at Garsdale.

Left: Another study of 5MT No. 5407 on the Cumbrian Mountain Pullman run-past of May 2nd, 1981. *(both Peter Fox)*

The star newcomer in 1980/1 to the fleet of locomotives handling the Cumbrian Mountain Express was 4-6-2 No. 46229 'Duchess of Hamilton', restored in B.R. crimson livery. Unfortunately the weather was never very kind on the days she put in an appearance but at least the clouds were above ground level when the Duchess paused at Garsdale on March 28th, 1981. *(Peter Fox)*

Viaducts large and small. Above: 'Flying Scotsman' crosses Lunds viaduct with the Bishop Treacy special on September 30th, 1978.

Left: Dandry Mire on March 25th, 1978, with 'Green Arrow' pulling away in fine style with The Norfolkman. *(both G. W. Morrison)*

'Black Fives' to the fore. Right: No. 5305, in pre-war lined black livery, crossing the Lunds on March 1st, 1980.
Below: Nos. 4767 'George Stephenson' and 5407 emerge from the short Shotlock tunnel on April 4th, 1981. *(both G. W. Morrison)*

CUMBRIAN
MOUNTAIN
EXPRESS
5305
L M S
5305

The backcloth of Wild Boar Fell has a distinctly bleak look as 5MT No. 5305 slogs up to Ais Gill with a ten-coach Cumbrian Mountain Express in March 1980. *(Peter Fox)*

AIS GILL

By contrast, spring is just round the
corner on May 2nd, 1981, as sister
engine No. 5407 bursts under the road
bridge with the Cumbrian Mountain
Pullman. *(Peter Fox)*

**Left: Lonely Ais Gill signal-box, a
typical Midland Railway structure.**
(British Railways)

CUMBRIAN
MOUNTAIN
EXPRESS
6201

Steam in the fells. Above: The memorable weather conditions of March 22nd, 1980, when blizzarding snow suddenly gave way to sunshine as No. 5305 thundered out of the whiteness. *(Peter Fox)*

Left: A thumbs-up sign from the driver of 'Princess Elizabeth' on September 4th, 1980. *(G. W. Morrison)*

SOUTHERN
850
CUMBRIAN
MOUNTAIN
EXPRESS
350

Left: 'Lord Nelson' on the final stages of the climb to Ais Gill summit on the last day of July 1980.

Right: 'Leander' shows signs of a badly burned smokebox door as she crosses Ais Gill viaduct on April 26th, 1980, the occasion when the locomotive made an out-and-back working to Carlisle in a single day. *(both G. W. Morrison)*

The Eden Valley

Mallerstang to Carlisle

As ever, without a trace of effort showing at the Kylchap, A4 No. 4498 'Sir Nigel Gresley' leaves the southern portal of Birkett tunnel on July 24th, 1980. *(David Wilcock)*

'Flying Scotsman' makes relatively light work of the climb out of the Eden valley towards Birkett tunnel during the glorious feast of steam that preceded the Rainhill celebrations of May 1980. *(Gordon Findlay)*

Another study of Gresley influence on the Settle & Carlisle. A4 No. 4498 approaches Hangman's Bridge, above Mallerstang, in the summer of 1980. *(David Wilcock)*

Contrasts at Kirkby Stephen. Below: 'Leander' passes the characteristic station buildings on July 3rd, 1980. The lack of any nearby habitation is another typically Settle & Carlisle feature.

Right: No. 4767 'George Stephenson' heads south in the freezing conditions of February 28th, 1981. The relatively new signal-box is just visible in the background. *(both G. W. Morrison)*

CUMBRIAN
MOUNTAIN
EXPRESS
4767

Left: Water crane at Appleby station. *(British Railways)*

Right: Returning to Falkirk after making an appearance at the 'Rocket 150' celebrations at Rainhill, 'Maude' passes derelict Newbiggin station with its light load of two former Caledonian Railway coaches on May 31st, 1980. *(David Wilcock)*

NATIONAL
GIROBANK
No 675
No 675

CUMBRIAN
MOUNTAIN
EXPRESS
46229

Scenes at Culgaith. Above: On March 1st, 1980, 5MT No. 5305 has just passed over the only level crossing on the Settle & Carlisle.

Left: 'Duchess of Hamilton' storms out of Culgaith tunnel on November 8th, 1980. *(both G. W. Morrison)*

SOUTHERN
850
CUMBRIAN
MOUNTAIN
EXPRESS
850

Left: 'Lord Nelson' in the pictur-
esque reaches of the Eden gorge
near Baron Wood, south of Armathwaite, on July 31st, 1980.

Right: 'Evening Star' on Sep-
tember 30th, 1978, en route from
Appleby to Armathwaite with
The Lord Bishop special. *(both
G. W. Morrison)*

Left: Merchant Navy No. 35028 'Clan Line' storms round the curve out of Armathwaite with an up special on September 30th, 1978.

Right: 'Duchess of Hamilton' has just passed on to Settle & Carlisle metals as she runs alongside the site of the former Durran Hill locomotive sheds on November 8th, 1980. *(both G. W. Morrison)*

'Sir Nigel Gresley' threads through the outskirts of Carlisle and passes the Cowans Sheldon crane plant on July 24th, 1980. *(David Wilcock)*

'Evening Star' at the north end of Carlisle Citadel station with The Border Venturer on May 13th, 1978. *(Derek Cross)*

Vintage Steam

Above: Midland Railway 0-6-0 at Settle station in 1914 at head of special train for army volunteers. *(A. Horner collection)*

Right: 4MT 2-6-2T No. 42472 coasts past Stainforth Sidings with a Garsdale - Hellifield local in July 1961. *(Derek Cross)*

The north portal of Stainforth tunnel in L.M.S. days with (above) unrebuilt Patriot No. 5501 emerging and (left) a 'Crab' 2-6-0 heading south. *(both D. Ibbotson)*

The dramatic view from the footplate of a Britannia class Pacific about to cross Ribblehead viaduct. *(Eric Treacy)*

Normal service will be resumed as soon as possible! Above: Bedlam at Blea Moor on August 11th, 1968, as 5MT 4-6-0s Nos. 44871 and 44781 make a photographic stop with what was then heralded as 'the last steam train on British Railways'. *(British Railways)*

Right: 8F No. 48149 snowed up at Dent in the winter of 1963; the 9F 2-10-0 is on a ballast train removing snow. *(Isaac Hailwood)*

48149

Even though the Garsdale water troughs were the highest in the world, they were relatively seldom photographed because of their inaccessible location. 'Crab' 2-6-0 No. 42819 is heading towards Rise Hill tunnel with an up freight. *(J. W. Armstrong)*

Another famed and now vanished feature of the Settle & Carlisle was Garsdale turntable, stockaded as a result of an engine being sent spinning round and round during a gale. D20 No. 62347 is being turned after working a Northallerton - Hawes - Garsdale train. *(J. W. Armstrong)*

Lower-quadrant signalling still in evidence as 5MT No. 45012 pounds through Garsdale with an up goods in February 1954. *(Real Photographs)*

A leisurely but delightful way to see the Settle & Carlisle was on the afternoon 'all-stations' from Bradford. Prior to being taken over by diesel units in 1966, it had a remarkable variety of motive power as instanced by this June 1965 view of the train crossing Dandry Mire viaduct behind begrimed 'Britannia' 4-6-2 No. 70002. *(Derek Cross)*

The summer Saturday Heads of Ayr to Leeds train emerges from the 106yd long Shotlock tunnel behind 5MT No. 44665 in July 1961. *(Derek Cross)*

Right: A 5MT tackles the last few yards of the climb to Ais Gill with an up freight — note the cattle wagon at the front of the train. *(J. W. Armstrong)*

Right: 2P 4-4-0 No. 459 heads a goods train past Ais Gill in 1929. *(Locomotive & General Railway Photographs)*

Opposite: Among the finest action photographs ever taken on the Settle & Carlisle is this study of Jubilee No. 45611 'Hong Kong' breasting Ais Gill summit with the up Thames-Clyde Express. It has often been reproduced but certainly bears repeating. *(W. Hubert Foster)*

44197
44197

Above: Trains pass at Kirkby Stephen in June 1962. 'Scot' 4-6-0 No. 46145 is in charge of the up Waverley, whilst 'Crab' 2-6-0 No. 42835 is ambling north with a mixed freight. *(Derek Cross)*

Opposite: 4F No. 44197 steams forth out of Birkett tunnel with an up goods in the early 1960s. *(P. J. C. Weston)*

'Compound' 4-4-0 No. 1069 near Cotehill in L.M.S. days — note the lower quadrant signals. *(E. E. Smith)*

The magnificence of a Midland Railway express is well captured in this view of 4-4-0 No. 998 heading round the curve on to the North Eastern at Carlisle with a train composed entirely of clerestory rolling stock. *(Real Photographs)*

A climb of over a thousand feet lies ahead for 4-4-0s Nos. 412 and 1071 as they ease out of Carlisle with an express which in those palmy days terminated at London St. Pancras. *(Real Photographs)*

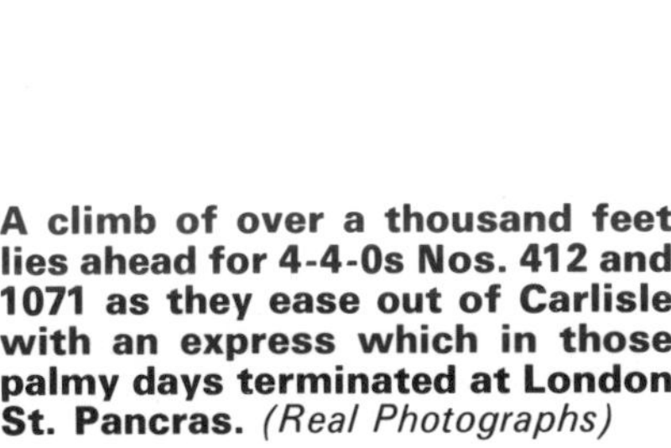

Left: One of the superb lamps of 5MT No. 5305 — a regular performer on the Cumbrian Mountain Express. *(Peter Fox)*

Chapter heading illustrations are as follows:
Page 3: Dent Head viaduct *(Stanley Bond)*; Page 5: 5MT No. 5305 at Steamtown, Carnforth, prior to working the Cumbrian Mountain Express *(Peter Fox)*; Page 6: The same train in charge of No. 4472 'Flying Scotsman' *(Peter Fox)*; Page 10: Horton-in-Ribblesdale station in 1952 *(Locomotive & General Railway Photographs)*; Page 24: Dent signal-box *(W. R. Mitchell)*; Page 32: Ais Gill summit sign *(British Railways)*; Page 50: Smardale viaduct *(W. R. Mitchell)*; Page 64: Hawes Junction station — later renamed Garsdale — about 1905 *(L&GRP)*